YOU CAN DO TO RAISE
YOUR SELF-ESTEEM

By the same author:

MAXIMUM SELF-ESTEEM:
The Handbook for Reclaiming
Your Sense of Self-Worth

52 THINGS
YOU CAN DO TO RAISE
YOUR SELF-ESTEEM

Jerry Minchinton

Arnford House, *Publishers*

Preassigned LCCN: 94-78712

ISBN 0-9635719-6-6

Arnford House is a division of The Arnford Corporation

Printed in the United States of America

10 9 8 7 6 5 4 3 2 1

CONTENTS

Acknowledgments

Both I and this book have been shaped by many positive influences. Among them, the writings of psychologist Albert Ellis, and the philosophies and schools of thought which encourage a reality-based world-view.

Help of a more immediate nature was provided by three caring, supportive people, who are also valued friends. Clif Bradley, a business associate for many years, read, re-read, and commented on all my drafts with extraordinary patience. Stacy Gilbert was generous enough to share her wit and insight with me, and to give me the benefit of her extensive knowledge of contemporary culture. I am grateful to Jean Names, who, besides being a font of wisdom and encouragement, also has the amazing talent of seeing more in you than you see in yourself. Thank you all for being the wonderful friends you are.

About Self-Esteem

At its simplest, good self-esteem means liking yourself and believing you deserve the good things in life as much as anyone else does. Since the subject is somewhat more involved than this, readers who would like a more thorough discussion are invited to read the author's *Maximum Self-Esteem: The Handbook for Reclaiming Your Sense of Self-Worth.*

Is self-esteem important? Very much so; it has a major effect on almost every part of your life. This includes your relationships, degree of self-confidence, choice of career, happiness, peace of mind, and even how much success you eventually achieve.

How do people develop poor self-esteem? All of us, while we were growing up, had unpleasant experiences that made us think badly of ourselves. But some of us had so many we unconsciously translated them into three core beliefs, which most of us believe to a greater or lesser degree. *First*, that we're powerless victims who have little to say about what goes on in our lives. *Second*, we're inadequate and in many ways don't measure up to others. *Third*, there is something innately "bad" about us.

Regaining good self-esteem isn't a mysterious process. More than anything else, it's a matter of revising your opinion of yourself. To do this, you learn to counter those incorrect core beliefs by emphasizing your control over your life, your personal adequacy, and your natural, inborn sense of self-worth.

What can you expect for your efforts if you're willing to spend some time improving your self-esteem? Well, how about increased social confidence, more satisfying relationships, and a feeling of cheerful cooperation with life, for starters? The biggest reward, you'll find, is your new self-image, because the person you become is a greatly "improved," much happier version of yourself.

How to Use This Book

There are many ways to approach the ideas you'll find here. You can: start at the beginning and work on them one at a time; do one a week for a year; choose one at random to give you a thought for the day; look for a specific heading for a particular type of situation, or use any other method you choose. If you'd like to choose by title, you can turn to the "Listing by Heading." Since each part stands alone, there's no preferred order for reading.

As simple as some of these suggestions are, each has the potential to make a significant improvement in your life. So if you're serious about improving your self-esteem, don't just read them, say "That's nice," and then go on your way. If you want more than a temporary lift, spend some time thinking about these ideas and how they apply to your life. As you'll notice, each section concludes with a "Key Thought," which summarizes its main idea. You can use these thoughts as ideas to ponder or as affirmations to prime your subconscious mind.

You may dislike or disagree with some of what you read here. If you do, you're in good company, because many of us would like to ignore some of these facts or pretend they're not true. Speaking from my own experience, the most difficult lessons have always been those I didn't *want* to learn. Unfortunately, that didn't make them any less true, so they kept repeating until I was forced to accept what they had to teach.

A word of caution: before putting the ideas contained in this book to use, I suggest you give careful thought to how they may affect your life situation. Even the most helpful tools can be harmful if used inappropriately or without consideration of the consequences.

I hope you enjoy this book.

52 THINGS
YOU CAN DO TO RAISE
YOUR SELF-ESTEEM

• • • • • • • • • • • • • • • •

Avoid punishing yourself for your mistakes. Don't call yourself names or tell yourself how stupid you are. That only reinforces the belief that you make poor choices, which makes you fearful and actually *increases* the chance of additional errors.

On the other hand, if you treat yourself gently when you make a mistake, you won't feel pressured and are less likely to make further mistakes. As an added bonus, by refusing to agonize over your not-so-perfect decisions, you remain open to learning how you made them and how to avoid similar mistakes in the future.

Poor choices are never intentional; no one writes "Make yourself miserable" at the top of the next day's agenda. Whenever you make a mistake, remember that errors are completely normal, that *everybody* makes them, and that *all* mistakes, even the most serious, are 100% forgivable.

KEY THOUGHT:

Being kind to myself when I make mistakes helps me avoid future errors.

Focus on your positive qualities and successes

· · · · · · · · · · · · · · · · · · ·

2   An unwritten law states: whatever we concentrate on expands. If you focus on another person's good qualities, they'll multiply. If you look for mistakes, you'll find plenty of them. If you frequently direct your attention to your good features and qualities, and to the happier parts of your life, you'll find they increase, too.

KEY THOUGHT:

Whatever I think about most increases.

☙ Learn to Say "No"

3 Some people have no hesitation about trying to convince you to do what they want, even if you find it distasteful or inconvenient. If you give in to their requests, you usually feel resentful, angry, and victimized.

Coming up with excuses to escape these situations is rarely helpful, because manipulators are often experts at countering even the most skillful of evasions. The best solution is the simplest: say, "I don't want to do it!"

Not only is it all right to say "No," to these people, you needn't give them a reason for doing so. Since they have no qualms about imposing on you, you need have none about refusing to be imposed on.

KEY THOUGHT:

Unless a task is truly my responsibility,
I have no obligation to do it.

🐝 Cheerfully reject any unkind remarks directed your way

•   •   •   •   •   •   •   •   •   •   •   •   •   •   •

4   Much as we might wish it weren't true, we sometimes encounter people who make rude comments to or about us, trying to make us feel bad. Individuals like these, to quote from an old song, "are more to be pitied than censured."

These unfortunates will try to put you down and make you feel bad, especially if they consider you an easy mark. They do this hoping you'll buy into their game and give them a feeling of superiority, thereby easing their self-esteem problems. If you *do* react to their comments with anger or embarrassment, then you've done just what they wanted: made *their* opinion of you more important than your own.

Until you are totally comfortable with your feelings about yourself, avoid people like this whenever you can. When you do encounter them, don't enter into their game by trying to think of a clever reply. Just smile and remain silent, or say something like "Oh, really?", and go on about your business. There's no reason to lower *your* self-esteem just to give a temporary boost to theirs.

KEY THOUGHT:

I refuse to feel bad about myself just to make someone else feel better.

Consider everyone you meet your equal

. . . .

5   While we were growing up, many of us were told we should "look up" to certain people. We were given the impression that knowledge, degrees, title, position, social standing, wealth, or some other distinction made them superior and deserving of special acclaim and attention.

It's true these things may make those who have them *different* from you, but it's also true they don't make them any *better*. Criteria like these are merely artificial distinctions on which to base respect and honor, and exceedingly poor ones at that. It makes as much sense to believe people deserve special recognition because they have extra-large thumbs or noses.

KEY THOUGHT:

Others' accomplishments and attributes don't make them more worthwhile or deserving of respect than I am.

Pay attention to feedback

⬡ **6**　It would be convenient if, at birth, each of us received a handbook titled *Everything You Need to Know To Avoid Mistakes*. Regrettably, that book is not yet on the market, so we all make quite a few mistakes, including some we become extremely unhappy about. What we overlook in our dejection is this vital fact: in most cases, mistakes are essential for learning.

Your errors, if you allow them to, can provide you with valuable feedback. Every time you make a mistake, you eliminate an incorrect answer or solution and move close to the correct one. And if you consistently grant yourself the freedom to make mistakes, you'll be rewarded by improved skills of all kinds, plus a significant increase in your overall chances of success.

KEY THOUGHT:

It is wise to consider every mistake a learning experience.

🐝 Be comfortably wrong

• • • • • • • • • • • • • •

___
7
___

Many of us are unwilling to admit it when we're wrong. That's because we blame ourselves for so much already that we rebel against adding even more fuel to the fire. At a deeper level of mind, we feel that if we can convince ourselves and others we're always right, we can avoid the feelings of "badness" that accompany being wrong.

But there's no reason to feel that way, so when you're wrong, admit it. You don't *have* to be right all the time. People don't get kicked off the planet just because they foul things up now and then. Being wrong occasionally doesn't make you a worse person any more than being right all the time makes you a better one.

Errors don't make you inadequate, merely human. Acknowledging them willingly is a mark of maturity and an indicator of healthy self-esteem.

KEY THOUGHT:

Right or wrong, I'm always worthwhile.

🌿 Make happiness a habit

• • • • • • • • • • • • • • • • •

8   To a large extent, how happy you are depends on your outlook on life. That's because happiness is a self-generated state of mind, not a mood that depends on having nice things happen to you.

Here's some startling news: you can increase the amount of happiness you feel with practice! Experiment by deliberately feeling happy for a five-minute period each day. Not being happy *because of* anything, but just to feel happy.

To do this, recall how you felt on one of the happiest days of your life, then bring that feeling into the present. If you do this regularly, you'll find it *is* possible to feel happy when you want to, and that you're feeling happy more often each day.

Happiness is like self-esteem: it's a personal responsibility. Although others can sometimes add to it, ultimately, how happy you are is up to you.

KEY THOUGHT:

My moods are my responsibility.

20

Stop calling yourself names

• • • • • • • • • • • • •

⑨ Keep your descriptive self-talk positive. .. you notice you're indulging in self-criticism for any reason, stop it! Like everyone else, you're often bound to fall short of perfection, but what's the point of making an issue of it?

Eliminate words like "dummy," "idiot," "scatter-brain," and "stupid" from your thoughts and speech. While you're doing this verbal housecleaning, get rid of any other unflattering terms, like "fatty," "clumsy," or "ugly."

Calling yourself names emphasizes what you *don't* have and unfairly ignores what you *do* have. And since there are usually plenty of volunteers willing to criticize you with absolutely no effort on your part, why add your voice to their chorus?

KEY THOUGHT:

I gain self-respect by using positive self-talk.

Find a job you enjoy

• • • • • • • • • • • • • • • • •

10 Doing work you resent is like punishment. When you dislike your job, it can be hard to get out of bed and even harder to make it through the day. And instead of taking pleasure in what you do, you try to block it out of your mind by concentrating on upcoming holidays, weekends, and paychecks.

Why remain in this kind of dead-end situation? If you don't like your work, change it; there's no point spending your day doing something you find unpleasant. You may not be able to make an immediate transition because of family responsibilities or financial considerations, but there is nothing to stop you from preparing for the future.

What can you do to get started? First, resolve to do whatever is necessary to get moving in the right direction. Then, choose your goal, make realistic step-by-step plans, and begin carrying them out.

When you love your work, everybody wins. You enjoy what you do, so you're happier and more pleasant to be around, while those who purchase what you provide receive a quality product or service crafted with love.

KEY THOUGHT:

I deserve work that brings me pleasure.

22

Never worry about the kind of impression you're making

• • • • • • • • • • • • • • • •

11 Remember this: anytime you're concerned about what people will think of *you*, they are probably just as concerned about what you will think of *them*.

KEY THOUGHT:

If the impression I make on others is important, I'm likely to make a better one if I relax and forget about it.

Improve your ideas about what you deserve

· · · · · · · · · · · · · · · · ·

12 Are you happy with the quality of your life? With your job, your relationships, and conditions at home? If you're not and you'd like to change them, you can.

In most cases, we aren't where we are by accident. The level of our self-esteem draws us into the kinds of relationships and situations we unconsciously feel we *deserve*, which may be vastly different from what we consciously *want*.

That's why people with healthy self-regard expect and generally receive, respect, cooperation, and friendliness from others. And why those who place too low a value on themselves often become involved in uncomfortable, unpleasant, or even abusive situations.

How can you create positive changes in your life? By concentrating on improving your self-esteem. As you do, you expand your concept of happiness. When you're genuinely convinced you deserve greater happiness, you'll take whatever safe, legal steps are necessary to bring it about.

KEY THOUGHT:

My value as a human being entitles me to the best life has to offer.

Accept yourself unconditionally — now

- - - - - - - - - - - - - - - -

13 We play the "If Game" with ourselves. We say and think things like, "I'd be a better person *if* I stopped doing this or *if* I started doing something else," or "I'd be more worthwhile *if* I had this or *if* I could do that." All these "ifs" deny that we're okay *right now* and postpone self-acceptance indefinitely, making us feel perpetually inadequate.

The fact is, you don't have to change anything to become okay, because you're all right just as you are. Regardless of any personal characteristics, you have always been and will always be a thoroughly worthwhile person in all respects.

In the interest of accuracy, what you *should* say to yourself is, "As a human being, I will always be 'work in progress.' I'm doing the best I possibly can at this time and as soon as I'm able to do better, I will."

KEY THOUGHT:

I'm perfectly worthwhile and acceptable just as I am.

🦋 Win back your freedom

• • • • • • • • • • • • • • • • •

14   Many of us, while we were growing up, got an exaggerated idea of the importance of others' opinions. Parents and other authority figures asked us questions like, "What will people say?", or "What will people think?" This led us to believe others' thoughts about us were of prime significance.

How does this affect us? By assigning too much value to what people think of us, we live for them, instead of ourselves. We do what they want, not what we want. We do what we believe will win others' applause, instead of what pleases us. The more importance we attach to people's opinions, the less freedom we have to do, say, and even *think* what we wish. Even worse, by giving excessive importance to others' opinions of us, we also rank ourselves second to them as a human being.

KEY THOUGHT:

The more importance I give others' opinions, the less freedom I have to live as I choose.

Enjoy some quality personal time every day

• • • • • • • • • • • • • • • • •

 15 Make an appointment with yourself each day. Set aside at least thirty minutes purely for the purpose of doing something you truly enjoy. It doesn't have to be spectacular or expensive. It can be as simple as reading a chapter from a novel, writing poetry, eating a favorite food, or just sitting quietly without doing anything. Whatever you choose, be sure it provides you with personal satisfaction or pleasure.

It's remarkably easy to neglect your own life when you feel overwhelmed by the demands of your job, family, or friends. By reserving a block of time for yourself daily, you create a reminder that you and your needs and wants are as important as anyone's.

KEY THOUGHT:

I deserve some time for myself each day.

🍂 Ask yourself why people tell you how badly you've hurt them

. . . .

16 Sometimes people have unrealistic expectations for your behavior, and if you don't do what they want, they let you know you've hurt their feelings. They accuse you of thoughtlessness, lack of consideration, or deliberate unkindness.

People who resort to this kind of behavior know that if you buy into their game, they've gained an emotional baseball bat to beat you with when it looks like you might step out of line. By pretending to be victims themselves, they try to victimize *you*. Their goal is to make you so uncomfortable you'll change your priorities and do as they wish. If you become ashamed and apologetic, they've won the game, which means in the future, you'll live more like they want you to.

Does anyone have a right to expect you to behave differently than you choose? Unless you have an agreement with others, or have led them to believe they have a license to control your behavior, the answer is a resounding NO. No one should expect anything from you other than pleasant, courteous, non-harmful conduct. There's no reason to ignore *your* preferences solely to please others.

*My own expectations for myself
are the most important.*

Be prepared to work for what you want

. . . .

17 Do you sometimes create elaborate plans for future achievements, and then feel unhappy and disappointed when they don't eventually appear? If this happens often, you may be omitting an essential ingredient from your plans.

While it's great to have dreams and think about the future, hardly anything happens just because you want it to. Much as we might like it to be otherwise, it usually takes more than wishing and hoping to turn desires into reality. If you are serious about reaching a particular goal, you're much more likely to be successful if you're willing to invest a substantial amount of personal energy in achieving it.

KEY THOUGHT:

If I want something, I'll probably have to earn it in one way or another.

❦ Give your own opinion of yourself top priority

. . . .

18 We tend to overvalue people's opinions of us and take their unflattering comments to heart. It's as though we believe their assessments of our character, behavior, or personality are both important and highly accurate. But how close to the truth are others' opinions of us likely to be?

Because people make judgements from within *their* frame of reference, rather than yours, their ideas about you are more apt to be wrong than right. Considering how little knowledge others actually have about your background and life experiences, how can they possibly understand why you are as you are and behave as you do? All they can do is judge you as they would judge themselves under similar circumstances.

Keep in mind that, for the most part, people's ideas about you are usually inaccurate. Unless others' feelings concerning you have a significant bearing on your welfare or livelihood, there's little reason to pay them any attention.

KEY THOUGHT:

I'm usually better off taking people's opinions of me with a grain of salt.

Be 100% positive one day a week

· · · · · · · · · · · · · · · · · ·

_____ Are you in the habit of complaining to yourself
19   when things don't go the way you'd like them
_____ to? And if you are, have you ever noticed it doing you any good?

Griping and whining may feel justified, but they just
make matters seem worse. Unless you do something to improve things, complaining about them only makes you
miserable and reinforces your victim status ("Why do these
things always happen to me?").

Choose one day a week to confront this habit. On
that day, no matter what happens, don't complain or
criticize. When you notice you're thinking an unhappy
thought, instead of pursuing it, immediately switch to a
pleasant subject.

This may take a little practice, and if you're a heavy-
duty complainer, you'll probably have to begin with a short
period of time. But once you learn to bypass negative
thoughts even briefly, you'll be amazed how much brighter
and more comfortable your life becomes.

KEY THOUGHT:

I am happier when I avoid unhappy thoughts.

Expect people to be different from you

· · · · · · · · · · · · · · · · · ·

20 Generally, we assume other people will act pretty much the same way we would. When they don't, we become angry, unhappy, or fearful. But unless you know others extremely well, you're as likely to be wrong as right if you attempt to predict their actions. Just as *your* behavior is shaped by your unique combination of heredity, background, and life experience, so is *theirs*. It is this individual uniqueness that sometimes makes others' actions as incomprehensible to you as yours are to them.

KEY THOUGHT:

People have good reasons for behaving differently than I do.

Decide how perfect "perfect" is

. . . .

 Perfectionists are not happy people. They do a lot of extra work because they believe nobody else can do things as well as they can. They agonize over making decisions. Because they continually look for mistakes, they always find them. Worst of all, they equate their ability to do everything perfectly with their worth as a person, which means they rarely think of themselves as first-class human beings.

There is a degree of perfection appropriate to every task. Brain surgery, for instance, takes quite a bit more than mowing a lawn. But the trick is to decide *ahead of time* exactly how well something must be done. Then, knowing just how good it needs to be, you can give it the attention it deserves.

As far as your feelings about yourself are concerned, your goal should be not to *do* everything perfectly, but to realize you don't *have* to!

KEY THOUGHT:

It's always smart to set realistic standards for myself.

. . . .

22 Avoid comparing yourself with other people. On the one hand, comparisons breed discontentment, and on the other, an false sense of superiority. Both hinder you from developing a realistic self-image.

When you compare yourself with others, typically you think of some people who are superior to you and others who are inferior. Then you feel bad because you're not as good as the one group, but cheer up because you're better than the other. Since the overall result is to leave you feeling inadequate, you'd save a lot of effort if you skipped the intermediate steps and simply felt bad to begin with.

This kind of comparison is never valid anyway, because you, like every other human being on this planet, are unique, with individual strengths, weaknesses, talents, and abilities. Your heredity, background, life experiences, and understanding combine to make you different from everyone else. This is neither good nor bad, it's just a fact.

KEY THOUGHT:

Since I am unique, it is pointless to compare myself with anyone else.

Don't let being different bother you

・　　・　　・　　・　　・　　・　　・　　・　　・　　・　　・　　・　　・　　・　　・

23　　We sometimes encounter people who want to convince us we're not worthwhile. Because we differ from them in certain respects, they consider us of little consequence. These "important" differences may be in how we look or act, our beliefs, religion, skin color, ethnic background, race, sexual orientation, gender, income, heredity, or in hundreds of other "inferiority indicators."

Why do people engage in this pathetic charade? Because if they can convince themselves they're better than others, they gain synthetic self-worth. By creating categories of supposedly inferior people, they elevate themselves in their own eyes. This would be like Saturn deciding it's a more valuable planet than Mars because it has rings.

No matter who tries to convince you otherwise, there are no guidelines for determining human value, just arbitrary decisions made by insecure people. Human worth isn't a commodity that can be measured by the yard or pound, it's something we receive at birth and keep until we die.

Whenever you're around people who try to make themselves look good by making you look bad, remember: no one can make you feel inferior without your consent.

KEY THOUGHT:

Nothing about me makes me better or worse than anyone else.

Avoid causing yourself unnecessary pain.

• • • • • • • • • • • • • • • • •

24 There is a rather bad joke that gives us some insight into the workings of our negative emotions. As the story goes, a man saw a small boy repeatedly hitting his thumb with a hammer. Finally, the man's curiosity got the better of him. "Why," he asked, "do you keep hitting your thumb when it obviously hurts you so much?" The boy replied: "Because it feels so good when I stop."

Despite its debatable humor, this story underlines an important fact: just as the boy caused his own pain with the hammer, we cause ourselves pain with our emotions.

We probably think emotional responses are pretty automatic: something happens and it causes us to react as we do. But that isn't how it works: emotions are strictly an inside job. When something happens, *you* decide you don't like it, then *you* beat yourself up with emotional pain.

If you don't admit to creating these painful feelings, you blame them on external causes and feel victimized, which doesn't solve a thing. On the other hand, if you accept responsibility for these states of mind, you gain an incredible power. Not only will you stop trying solutions that never work, you'll discover you no longer need rely on anything outside yourself to determine your mood.

KEY THOUGHT:

I can avoid a lot of pain by not hurting myself.

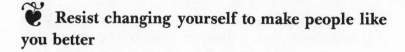 **Resist changing yourself to make people like you better**

• • • • • • • • • • • • • • •

25 Sometimes, for reasons unknown to us, people make it obvious they dislike us. When they do, we typically assume we're at fault and wonder what we can do to fix things. We ask ourselves, "What am I doing wrong?"

What we need to ask is, "Why do I automatically assume it's *my* obligation to change when someone doesn't like me?" The solution to the problem of others disliking you isn't changing yourself to make people like you better, it's understanding that it's neither possible nor necessary to please everyone.

KEY THOUGHT:

I don't have to change to make people like me.

Cease identifying yourself with your actions

• • • • • • • • • • • • • • • • •

26 You are not what you do. Having done "bad" things doesn't make you a bad person, just someone who, on occasion, has made unwise decisions.

This brings up the question of motivation: Why *do* we behave as we do? Sometimes we act impulsively, without considering the consequences of our actions. Other times, we're unclear about our reasons and act without knowing or understanding why. Then, of course, many unwise actions don't seem unwise at the time — they seem like the best things to do and only later do we discover they weren't.

Keep this fact in mind: Your actions are totally unrelated to your worth or value as a person; what you do is not the same as what you are. Just as you do not become a good person by avoiding mistakes, you do not become a bad person by making them.

KEY THOUGHT:

I am thoroughly worthwhile even though I've done unwise things.

🐝 Emphasize the many correct decisions you make

• • • • • • • • • • • • • • •

27 Instead of allowing your mistakes to overwhelm you, think about the numerous *good* choices you've made throughout your life. Congratulate yourself on past successes and emphasize your wise decisions.

From a practical viewpoint, just being alive from day to day requires you to make literally thousands of judgement calls. With all these opportunities for error, it is unreasonable to expect *all* your choices to be perfect.

The truth is, you are right far more often than you're wrong. Compared to the huge number of wise, life-enhancing decisions you make every day, your errors are remarkably few.

KEY THOUGHT:

I make far more good decisions than bad ones.

• • • • • • • • • • • • • • • • •

28   If you believe it's important that others have good feelings about you, you're probably, to paraphrase a well-known song, "looking for approval in all the wrong places."

When you place too much value on people's opinions of you, you allow them to affect your feelings about yourself. If you rely on others' approval to make you feel good, you'll feel bad when they withdraw it; by desiring people's praise, you automatically make yourself vulnerable to their blame.

Others' good opinions are important when it's a matter of survival, of course, but when it comes to making you feel good about yourself, they're definitely not. You'll save an enormous amount of emotional wear and tear when you genuinely understand that the only approval you *must* have is your own.

KEY THOUGHT:

The approval I need most comes from inside me, not from others.

🍒 Take charge of your health

· · · · · · · · · · · · · · · · ·

29 What can you do to take charge of your health? Literally hundreds of things. There is an abundance of non-technical books on health and nutrition, books that tell you how to identify, eliminate and prevent many unhealthy conditions. There are also countless classes, videos, and films that teach how to develop and maintain optimum health. And don't overlook good health basics like quitting smoking, eating sensibly, and getting plenty of rest and exercise.

There are four good reasons you should consider your health primarily *your* responsibility. *First*, medical professionals have to spend most of their time repairing the damage we've done to ourselves, so they have little time to tell us how to avoid problems. *Second*, no one else has as much at stake as you. *Third*, you are the only one who is in a position to monitor your health and be aware of the many details of your life that affect your physical wellbeing. *Fourth*, by taking an active part in maintaining good health, you automatically gain greater control over your life, and by doing so, increase your self-esteem.

KEY THOUGHT:

My health is primarily my own responsibility.

44

Smile when you're criticized

. . . .

30 Few things reveal the state of our self-esteem so clearly as the way we respond to others' criticism. When we don't like ourselves well enough, we often interpret people's negative appraisals as personal attacks, as disapproval of ourselves as a human being.

When someone criticizes you, remember these facts:

1) You may be able to learn from the critique, and if you *are* doing something wrong, it's in your best interest to know it;

2) Criticism of something you *do* isn't a judgement of you as a person;

3) Even if someone *does* mean their remarks as a personal attack, why should you endorse their efforts by cooperating with them?

KEY THOUGHT:

It's to my advantage to accept criticism with a relaxed, open-minded attitude.

🍎 Do your own thinking and make your own decisions

• • • • • • • • • • • • • • •

31 There are always plenty of people willing to give you free advice or make up your mind for you. Despite a conspicuous lack of success in their own lives, some individuals feel qualified to advise you about your life. But even if your would-be advisers are successful and happy, there are important reasons why letting them make your decisions isn't a good idea.

Since no one is as intimately acquainted with your life as you are, others' solutions may not meet your needs as well as your own would. Second, when other people make decisions for you, matters often turn out the way *they* want them to, which may be quite different from what *you* want. The last and most compelling reason, though, is if you allow others to make decisions for you, you will never learn to make them yourself

There's nothing wrong with listening to others' advice, of course. Ultimately, though, *you* are the one who must live with the consequences of your actions, regardless of who suggested you make them. Even if your decisions aren't always perfect, it's better to make mistakes and learn from them than to rely continually on others' judgement.

KEY THOUGHT:

It is in my best interest to make my own decisions.

Accept compliments graciously

· · · · · · · · · · · · · · ·

32 It isn't modesty that causes that uncomfortable feeling you get when someone compliments you, it's self-consciousness. When you're praised, you become embarrassed because you don't believe you deserve it.

As children, most of us learned it wasn't okay to say good things about yourself; People considered those who did conceited or vain. As a result, we tend to shy away from others' favorable comments. It's time, however, to update our childhood instruction.

There's nothing wrong with acknowledging you've done a good job. When people congratulate you on doing well, you don't have to say "Yes, I *was* wonderful, wasn't I?" Just accept their compliments with good grace. Don't try to downplay your abilities or skills by saying things like "Oh, it was nothing," or "I didn't do as well as I should have." Disagreeing with people who compliment you is the same as telling them they're stupid or lacking in judgement.

The next time someone generously offers you praise for your accomplishments, be generous in return and accept it with a sincere "Thank you." Chances are you deserve it.

KEY THOUGHT:

It's okay to admit I did a good job.

🍒 Become flexible

• • • • • • • • • • • • • • • • •

33   Life, we believe, would be greatly improved if only people would change their behavior and be more like we want them to be. But despite our begging, complaining, or strong-arm tactics, most people flatly refuse to change just because we want them to. And those that *do* change seldom stay that way for long unless we make it worth their while.

Ultimately, and wisely, we finally realize that most of our problems with people won't go away until we stop thinking of them as problems. Thus, we learn one of the unalterable truths of life: Rather than wasting time trying to coerce others into doing what you want, it's usually quicker, more realistic, and longer-lasting to simply adjust your attitude.

KEY THOUGHT:

I can eliminate many non-threatening problems from my life merely by changing my attitude about them.

🍎 Value your ideas

· · · · · · · · · · · · · · ·

34 When you are in non-threatening situations, say what you *really* think, instead of what you believe others want you to say. That doesn't mean you should knowingly make unkind or unflattering remarks to or about others. But it *does* mean your opinion is at least as important as that of anyone else.

It doesn't matter whether others agree with you. Even if your ideas are different or conflict with what most people think, that doesn't lessen their importance or your right to make them known.

The next time you're inclined to agree with someone purely to please him, don't. Besides making you feel dishonest, compromising your truth and ideals will never win you any friends worth having. When you genuinely disagree with someone, <u>say so</u>.

KEY THOUGHT:

My ideas are as important as those of anyone else.

❦ Learn to do something you've been having someone else do for you

• • • • • • • • • • • • • • • •

35   Add a new skill to your store of abilities. It doesn't have to be a major project, like remodeling a house. It can be as simple as changing a flat tire, giving yourself a manicure, balancing a checkbook, or making scrambled eggs.

The idea is not to save money (although that has a certain appeal to many of us), but to build self-reliance. Once you've learned your new skill and a situation arises where you can't find someone to do the job for you, you can do it yourself and avoid feeling like a victim.

Knowledge gained through practical experience provides a big boost to your feelings of competence and personal adequacy. And equally important, it contributes directly to your feeling of being in control of your life.

KEY THOUGHT:

*The more I learn to do for myself,
the more control I gain over my life.*

❧

Don't take any kind of competition seriously

. . . .

36 Supposedly, competition builds character and self-confidence. In fact, it fails miserably at both. What it *really* does is cause feelings of inferiority and loss of self-esteem for the majority of people who compete.

How can it not, when by its very design competition means that more people must lose than win? And any activity that causes a majority of us to feel inferior to others can only be described as incredibly damaging.

The real danger of competition is that so many of us relate our value as a person to whether we lose or win. Losing, which is what we do most of the time, not only doesn't make us feel better, it makes us feel worse! We brand ourselves second-, third-, or fourth-rate and consider ourselves losers in the bargain.

Unless winning will provide you with a reward that greatly improves your life, competition is best ignored. If you *do* compete, and do so for anything other than the pleasure of playing, you're missing out on what little benefit competitive situations *can* provide.

KEY THOUGHT:

I'm always a thoroughly worthwhile person, whether I win or lose.

. . . .

37 Take an active part in the political process. It's an excellent way to weaken the "victim" mind-set and increase your feelings of control. Here are some of the many things you can do:

- Call or write your lawmakers: tell them your concerns and let them know what you expect from them.

- Talk to candidates for office: ask them their position on matters that affect you.

- Join a political action group: take an active role in changing laws and policies with which you disagree.

- Become a candidate yourself: if you feel you can do a better job than those currently in office, you could be right.

- Vote: learn about the issues and individuals involved in upcoming elections, then make your feelings about them known in the voting booth.

Life would be considerably easier if all politicians and elected officials were smart, honest, and ethical. Since they're not, we must become involved in government ourselves if we want our wishes to be respected. If we are indifferent to the political process, we may wake up one morning to find some of the liberties we've taken for granted have been legislated out of existence.

KEY THOUGHT:

*Government represents me best when
I take an active part in it.*

Consider your own needs most important

· · · · · · · · · · · · · · · · · ·

38 Steer clear of martyrdom. Idealistic people may try to convince us we should be willing to make sure others have plenty, even when it means we don't have enough ourselves. This may sound noble, but engaging in self-sacrifice means you believe other people and their needs are more important than your own, which is nonsense.

No matter how you look at it, it's impossible for anyone to be more important than you are, because there's no rating system by which human worth can be measured. We are *all* equally important and so are our needs.

KEY THOUGHT:

My needs are as important as those of anyone else.

Look straight ahead

· · · · · · · · · · · · · · · · ·

 We humans are a self-contradictory lot. In our minds we designate certain people as important, because they're wealthy, titled, hold degrees, or have something else somewhat uncommon about them. Then, once we've promoted them to the rank of Superior People, we complain because we think they look down on us! This makes as much sense as pouring water over your head and complaining because you're wet.

The solution to this problem is simple, because no one can look *down* on you unless you're looking *up* at them. Since you're the one who made these people bigger than life, restore them to life-size. Realize that whatever it is that makes them *different* from you doesn't make them any *better*. People, when all is said and done, are just people.

KEY THOUGHT:

I am neither more nor less important than anyone else.

❧

🍂 Say "No" to guilt

· · · · · · · · · · · · · · · ·

40 Guilt is a toxic, damaging emotion because it emphasizes your mistakes, rather than your successes. Even worse, this painful feeling wrongly makes you deny your innate sense of worth.

It would be one thing if we could just experience guilt for a few minutes and be done with it, but that's seldom how it works. Instead, many of us experience *chronic guilt* and feel its nagging presence daily.

Guilt isn't a natural emotion, in the sense that we're born with the ability to feel it. We were taught to experience it as children, by authority figures who used it to manipulate us into behaving as they wished. By encouraging us to associate guilt and shame with behavior they disliked, they tried to insure we would always behave as they wanted us to.

Unfortunately, because of this training we often feel guilty even when we've done nothing genuinely or intentionally harmful. And if we think about it, we'll realize much of what we *do* feel guilty about is simply the personal preferences and idiosyncrasies of our guilt teachers.

Is guilt useful? It's true it can convince you not to repeat certain kinds of actions. But sincere regret teaches the same lesson — without beating you up emotionally to do it.

In the final analysis, guilt serves no useful purpose. Besides causing a great deal of emotional pain, what it does best is convince you you're worthless. That alone is sufficient reason to discontinue feeling it.

KEY THOUGHT:

Guilt works against me, not for me.

Think of yourself as a valuable human being

• • • • • • • • • • • • • • • • •

41 Avoid the mistake of believing your value as a human being has any relationship to how accomplished, intelligent or wealthy you are. Although what you can do and what you own may affect your income, they have no bearing on your importance or worth as a person.

You don't have to do anything special to acquire the maximum amount of human worth; it's yours by virtue of being born into this world. Nothing you do can add to or subtract from your intrinsic value as a human being.

KEY THOUGHT:

I'm worthwhile because I exist, not because of anything I do or own.

Forgive yourself for all your mistakes

• • • • • • • • • • • • • • • • • •

42 Why do we take our mistakes so very, very seriously? Because we're in the habit of blaming ourselves. So much so, in fact, that many of us blame ourselves for things we couldn't possibly have prevented and even for problems we had no part in creating.

Yes, it's true you make mistakes, but so what? Why beat yourself up for being just like everybody else? None of us ever become so wise we do everything flawlessly. Since we have so little knowledge on which to base our judgements, mistakes are inevitable.

It is truly said, "To understand is to forgive." When you genuinely understand why you make mistakes, there is no longer any question of blaming yourself. Instead, you realize that, based on what you know at the time, you *always* make the best decision you can. That is all any of us can do.

KEY THOUGHT:

It's wise to forgive myself for all my mistakes, because I make none of them intentionally.

❦ Interpret every event positively

· · · · · · · · · · · · · · · · · ·

 During the time we're growing up, we develop definite ideas about what makes a situation good or bad. What's interesting about this is that someone raised in another family or culture, with different beliefs and traditions, and different social and moral codes, may interpret events just the opposite of the way we do.

This makes it clear that all situations are essentially neutral in character — that is, they are neither good nor bad in themselves. While certain events may *seem* positive or negative, it's only because we've chosen to look at them that way.

If we believe a certain kind of happening is inherently negative or unpleasant, we search for data to support that belief. If, instead, we choose to think of it as positive or favorable, we collect evidence to support *that* belief. In both cases we can find "proof" our belief is correct, which demonstrates that we generally find what we look for.

That's why it's vital to create fresh interpretations for circumstances that ordinarily distress you. If you view them positively you're far more likely to enjoy a pleasant outcome. This won't make an uncomfortable situation go away, but realizing you can derive benefits from it makes it easier to accept.

From the standpoint of self-esteem, being able to find positive aspects in everything that happens to you is even more important. By deliberately choosing to emphasize the favorable side of every situation, you put the role of victim behind you and quietly assume control.

KEY THOUGHT:

It is always to my advantage to interpret events positively.

Forget any bad feelings you have about others

· · · · · · · · · · · · · · · · · · ·

When we have an unresolved disagreement or
44 feel we've been treated unfairly, we tend to have
hard feelings toward those we consider responsi-
ble. We're justified, we insist, in feeling bitter toward them.

But ultimately, a grudge hurts the one who carries it
more than it does anyone else. The negative feelings you
generate with an unforgiving attitude have a harmful effect
on your health and disposition. Even worse, by dwelling on
unhappy incidents from the past, you attract even more
unpleasant experiences into your life.

Of course, unless there are practical reasons for it,
you don't have to be especially friendly to those with whom
you've had problems. But by refusing to forgive and forget,
you deny your strength and flexibility, emphasize your feelings of helplessness, and reinforce your belief that you're a
victim, instead of someone in control.

KEY THOUGHT:

Having negative feelings about others
harms me more than it does them.

Become a problem-solver

· · · · · · · · · · · · · · · · ·

45   Whenever you experience a problem, ask yourself this question: at what point in the past would making a different decision have allowed me to avoid the problem altogether? In other words, what could you have done differently that would have prevented what happened from happening?

This exercise isn't intended to make you feel guilty, but to make you aware that *you* possess the power to prevent many future difficulties. By tracing your problems backward, you discover many opportunities where, by behaving differently, you could have bypassed many unpleasant situations.

You may find this idea hard to accept if you're in the habit of blaming your predicaments on externals. But if you *are* willing to admit you're responsible for many of your problems, you'll find you have fewer of them to contend with in the future.

KEY THOUGHT:

I am the best qualified person to solve my problems.

🍃 Stand up for your rights

· · · · · · · · · · · · · · · · · ·

46 If you haven't discovered it already, you'll find there are people who believe they know what is best for everyone else. They've convinced themselves they're smarter or more moral than you and that their ideas of what's good for you are better than your own.

You can find these individuals in every kind of occupation. If they're involved in creating laws or policies, they attempt to make them reflect their personal beliefs and principles, which may be vastly different from your own.

People like these don't care how inconvenient or disagreeable you might find some of their ideas, or how much they might violate your individual rights. Their only real concern is promoting their personal agenda.

Because of their colossal egotism, people like these ignore a vitally important fact: it is your right to live as you see fit, as long as you don't interfere with others' rights to do the same. Beyond that, what you do is no one's business but your own.

Does it really need saying that those who believe they have the right to tell you how to live are badly misguided? And that you are even more so if you let them?

KEY THOUGHT:

It is my right to live any way I choose as long as I respect others' rights to do the same.

Rely mostly on yourself

• • • • • • • • • • • • • • • •

47 While there will be times when you have no choice but to count on others, the person you should depend on most is yourself. By allowing people to do things for you that you can do yourself, not only do you remain dependent, you often have to settle for much less than you want.

Interestingly, increasing your self-reliance often leads to better relationships because you're free to accept people for what they are, instead of for what they can do for you.

KEY THOUGHT:

It is wisest to depend on myself more than others.

Accept all your thoughts as perfect

· · · · · · · · · · · · · · · · · · · ·

48 We've learned to characterize some of our thoughts as bad or dirty, so we recoil from them with shame and embarrassment. We feel guilty about other kinds of thoughts, and call ourselves mean, unkind, or sacrilegious for thinking them. We say things to ourselves like, "That's disgusting! Why am I thinking that?" We behave as though we have a split personality, with a Good Me whose job is to restrain the Bad Me when it steps out of line.

But don't blame yourself for anything you think. *All* your thoughts are legitimate; you think what you do for perfectly good reasons. Your heredity, background, life experiences, and other factors team up to produce the ideas that populate your mind. Having sound reasons for your thoughts doesn't mean you're free to act on them all, because doing so could cause problems. It *does* mean you shouldn't condemn yourself for mentally expressing *any* kind of idea, no matter how ugly a label you've learned to attach to it.

In truth, everyone has a garbage pit of sorts in their minds. Unhappily for them, many people try to disown the thoughts that come from theirs. It's unwise to deny any part of your life or yourself, however, because pretending something doesn't exist won't make it go away.

The wisest course is to acknowledge that your thoughts _are_ your thoughts. Then, with quiet acceptance and without judging their suitability, expose them to the cleansing light of day.

KEY THOUGHT:

*I accept every thought I think as a valid
part of me that needs expression.*

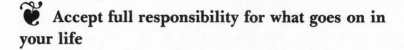 **Accept full responsibility for what goes on in your life**

• • • • • • • • • • • • • •

49 Don't blame God, fate, or other people when things don't happen the way you want them to. Your life and relationships will improve immensely when you realize that, in one way or another, most of what happens to you is the result of your actions or lack of them.

At first this seems like terrible news, because it requires you to assume a great deal of responsibility. But once you fully accept this fact, you become aware that you have vastly more control over your life than you imagined.

KEY THOUGHT:

By accepting responsibility for my life,
I gain greater control over it.

🐝 Accept blame only when you deserve it

● ● ● ● ● ● ● ● ● ● ● ● ● ● ● ●

50 While we were growing up, most of us were told we had the power to hurt others' feelings. Since we noticed at times that people became upset when we did or said certain things, we assumed this was true. We have been paying for that mistake ever since.

It *is* true people sometimes respond negatively to what we do. They do this by choice and habit, though, not because they have to. If our actions genuinely have the power to make people unhappy, they should make *everybody* unhappy, instead of just some. As you know, this isn't how it works.

Unless you deliberately set out to anger or disturb people, you have no obligation to accept blame for their reactions. It's difficult enough taking responsibility for your own emotional states, without adding the unnecessary and undeserved burden of others'.

KEY THOUGHT:

Others are responsible for their emotions, just as I am for mine.

Ask yourself whose life you're really living

• • • • • • • • • • • • • • • •

51 Sometimes we unknowingly become victims of others' expectations, and as a result, spend a great deal of time doing things we find disagreeable. If we're too wrapped up in our activities to notice, we mindlessly follow along without questioning the situation.

During the next month, set aside half an hour each week to take a long look at your life and ask yourself some questions. Is the job you're in one you enjoy, or one someone else felt was best for you? Do you spend your leisure time in pursuits that give you pleasure, or in activities that bore you stiff? In short, is living as you do *your* idea or someone else's?

Few of us can spend our lives entirely as we choose, because financial considerations and other obligations usually make it impossible. But if you discover you spend most of each day living out plans others have made for you, it's definitely time to begin living some dreams of your own.

KEY THOUGHT:

*It's important to live my life as I want,
not as others expect me to.*

Think and speak kindly of others

. . . .

52 Although thinking and speaking critically of others may provide us with a little entertainment or a temporary jolt of superiority, it is a dangerous pastime. Like complaining, fault-finding can easily become a habit, an unpleasant tendency that alienates friends and creates enemies.

The most hazardous part of dwelling on others' shortcomings is that fault-finding seems to take on a life of its own. It continuously searches for victims, and when no other target is available, goes to work on *you*. As a result, even though you may begin by directing your criticism at others, you end up making harsh judgements about yourself and eventually become your own worst enemy.

KEY THOUGHT:

I am the one who benefits most from thinking and speaking kindly of others.

❦ ❦ ❦

Listing by Heading

Recommended Reading

Arapakis, Maria, *Softpower! How to Speak Up, Set Limits, and Say No Without Losing Your Lover, Your Job, or Your Friends.* New York: Warner Books, Inc., 1990.

Ellis, Albert, Ph.D., and Becker, Irving M., Ed.D., *A Guide to Personal Happiness.* North Hollywood, CA: Wilshire Book Company, 1982.

Ellis, Albert, Ph.D., and Harper, Robert A., Ph.D., *A New Guide to Rational Living.* N. Hollywood, CA: Wilshire Book Company, 1975.

Hoff, Benjamin, *The Te of Piglet.* New York: Dutton, 1992.

Hoff, Benjamin, *The Tao of Pooh.* New York: Viking Penguin, Inc., 1982.

Keyes, Ken, Jr., *Handbook to Higher Consciousness,* Fifth Edition. Coos Bay, OR: Center for Living Love, 1975.

Kranzler, Gerald D., *You Can Change How You Feel: A Rational-Emotive Approach.* Eugene, OR: RETC Press, 1974.

Minchinton, Jerry, *Maximum Self-Esteem: The Handbook for Reclaiming Your Sense of Self-Worth.* Vanzant, MO: Arnford House, 1993.

Ming-Dao, Deng, *365 Tao: Daily Meditations.* San Francisco: Harper Collins San Francisco, 1992.

Seligman, Martin E.P., Ph.D., *Learned Optimism: How to Change Your Mind and Your Life*. New York: Pocket Books, 1990.

Seligman, Martin E.P., Ph.D., *What You Can Change and What You Can't: The Complete Guide to Successful Self-Improvement*. New York: Alfred A. Knopf, 1994.

Sills, Judith, Ph.D., *Excess Baggage: Getting Out of Your Own Way*. New York: Viking Penguin, 1993.

Weil, Andrew, M.D., *Natural Health, Natural Medicine: A Comprehensive Manual for Wellness and Self-Care*. Boston, MA: Houghton Mifflin Company, 1990.

About the Author

An accomplished musician, Jerry Minchinton performed professionally for a number of years before founding a mail processing company. After guiding the firm through twelve years of steady growth, he withdrew from his executive position to devote more time to the study of self-esteem.

He became interested in self-esteem when he and his business partner decided to use it as the basis of a pre-employment test. In the course of preparing the test, his study of self-esteem brought about a remarkable improvement in his own feelings of self-worth. This convinced him, not only that good self-esteem was highly important, but that achieving it was considerably simpler than is commonly believed.

Jerry earned his B.A. (with Highest Honors) and M.A degrees from Eastern Washington University, and then continued his education with doctoral studies at Florida State University. He is a member of the National Council for Self-Esteem and American MENSA.

For additional copies of this book, contact your local bookstore or order directly from the publisher.

Order Form

Telephone: Call 417·261·2559. Please have your VISA or Mastercard ready.
FAX: 417·261·2559.

Money orders: Arnford House; Route 1, Box 27; Vanzant, MO 65768.

Please send me:

_____ copies of *52 Things You Can do to Raise Your Self-Esteem* at $6.50 each _____

_____ copies of *Maximum Self-Esteem* at $14.95 each _____

Add $2.95 shipping for the first book, plus $1.00 for each additional book to the same address. Shipping _____

Missouri residents please add 6% tax per copy.   Tax _____

TOTAL ENCLOSED _____

Please allow 4 to 6 weeks for shipping.

Name:_____

Address:_____

City & State:_____ Zip: _____

Payment:

☐ Check   ☐ Money Order   ☐ VISA   ☐ Mastercard

Card number:_____

Name on card:_____ Exp. date:____ / ____

Signature:_____ Date:____ / ____ / ____